A PARCEL OF G(

Letters from Aus
from Ellen Re

This is the story of one of Australia's Pioneer Women, who spent most of her life in the gold fields of Bendigo.

In 1841, aged only 19, Ellen Suter fled poverty and squalor in the back-streets of Portsmouth and set off alone to live in the new colony of Victoria on the other side of the world.

In Melbourne, she met and married James Read, a settler from Ipswich, Suffolk, more than twenty years her senior. Over the next 20 years she bore him fourteen children, only five of whom survived.

Her story has been pieced together from the accidental discovery of seven letters written between 1853 and 1875 to her brother, William Suter, a papermaker in Headley, Hampshire.

To all those Pioneer Women
who created homes in far-off lands.

About the Author:

Joyce Stevens, née Suter, was born in Headley in 1914. Educated at the Holme School in Headley and then Eggars Grammar School, Alton, she went on to teach in Alton and Wrecclesham. She met her husband-to-be in Headley—he was a young teacher at the Holme School—but by the time they married in 1942 he had joined the Royal Air Force. Sadly, he was killed eight months later.

With altered circumstances, she completed her degree, became Head of the English Department in a local Comprehensive School, and made teaching her life career.

She lived for 90 years in the same house in Headley in which she was born. As the only child of Percy and Nell, this branch of the family name will die out, so she renamed the house *Suters* in 1971.

Joyce died peacefully on 12th August 2007 aged 93.

A Parcel of Gold for Edith

Joyce Stevens

A Parcel of Gold for Edith
First published 2001
Reprinted with minor additions 2002, 2007

Typeset and published by John Owen Smith
19 Kay Crescent, Headley Down, Hampshire GU35 8AH
Tel/Fax: 01428 712892
E-mail: wordsmith@headley1.demon.co.uk

ISBN 978-1-873855-36-2 (1-873855-36-2

Printed and bound by CPI Antony Rowe, Eastbourne

Edith Suter (1859–1939)

Descendants of William SUTER of Portsea (1783–1827)

1 William SUTER 1783–1827   *Note: Some dates are conjectural*
 +Frances CHIVERTON 1796–1863
 2 Amelia SUTER 1816–???
 2 William SUTER 1817–1906

<table>
<tr><td>Variations in spelling of surnames on source documents:—</td></tr>
<tr><td>SUTER   READ
SOUTER   REID
SOWTER</td></tr>
</table>

  +Eliza CHIVERTON 1823–1871
  3 George SUTER 1852–???
  3 William SUTER 1855–1904
   +Mary Ann SUTTON 1859–1942
   4 Percy SUTER 1886–1944
    +Nellie Mary SEAR 1886–1971
    5 Joyce Mary Eileen SUTER 1914–2007
    +Robert Plowden Weston STEVENS 1912–1942
  3 Edith SUTER 1859–1939
 2 Emma SUTER 1819–???
 2 Helen (Ellen) SUTER 1822–1882
  +James READ 1800–1888
  3 *Two Unnamed* READ c.1843 & 1844
  3 William James READ 1845–1924
  3 Frances (Fanny) Emma READ 1847–1873
   +Charles COOK 1841–1887
   4 Emma Ada COOK 1867–???
   4 Frances Sarah COOK 1868–???
   4 Martha COOK 1869–1890
   4 Susan COOK 1870–1873
   4 Charles James COOK 1873–1874
  3 Elizabeth Susan READ 1848–1882
  3 John Suter READ 1850–c.1857
  3 George Edwin READ c.1853
  3 Walter John Suter 'Ginger' READ 1855–1942
   +Susan Jane HARRISON 1857–1941
   4 Thomas 'Tonty' Edgar READ 1895–1974
   4 *Five other children, all died young*
  3 Ada Louise READ (twin) 1857–1863
  3 Arthur Benjamin READ (twin) 1857–1857
  3 Alice Ellen READ (twin) 1860–1860
  3 James READ (twin) 1860–1860
  3 Lilian READ (twin) 1862–1862
  3 Rosetta READ (twin) 1862–1950
   +James NANCARROW
   4 Albert Stephen NANCARROW 1887–1946
   4 Gladys May NANCARROW 1893–1960
    + William John Thomas BRAY
    5 Elsie May BRAY 1919–
    5 Mervyn Douglas Smilan BRAY 1920–1921
 2 Edwin SUTER (twin) 1827–???
 2 Emma Ann SUTER (twin) 1827–1866
  +Charles Rishman BAKER
  3 Fanny BAKER (& others)

Contents

৩১ ৩১ ৩১

Illustrations & Maps

ᘔᘔᘔ

Front cover: Edith Suter

Introduction

❧❧❧

Great aunt Edith's old bureau had become something of a legend in our family. From early childhood I had heard how upset she was by the persistence of a second-hand dealer from Reading who, on sporadic visits to our area, tried to persuade her to sell it to him—and the grown-ups marvelled that she always refused, for she had constant money worries.

There was the upkeep of our ancient cottage, at that time divided into three parts—we lived at the south end and she at the north, and only the middle part, the home of the village cobbler, brought her in any rent. In addition she owned two 'modern' cottages, Nos. 1 & 2 Southview down Rogers' Lane. Ironically these had been built by her father William in 1896 as a source of income for her when he died—for as a lonely maiden lady who had never had to earn her living, she would have had no other means, and old age pensions were unheard of in those days. He died in 1906, but the properties became nothing but an expense to her, being inhabited by sitting tenants paying a very small rent. She was constantly being called upon to replace a kitchen range, paint the outside, mend the roof, and so on.

So why wouldn't she sell her old bureau? A shabby, ugly, piece of furniture, was the opinion of Gran, her sister-in-law. The money would be much more useful.

Then, in 1939, she died aged 81. The cottages were left to my father, and I remember various pieces of her furniture, including the bureau, being carried along the back path of our cottage from the north end to the south.

For the first time, we realised what a treasure we had inherited. The outside of the bureau was indeed shabby, but the inside revealed a number of prettily-shaped pigeon-holes, secret drawers, sliding document compartments and adjustable shelves.

Great aunt Edith's bureau, in which Ellen's letters were found

And it was, of course, choc-a-bloc with the accumulation of several life-times. Great grandfather, who could read and write, had been a great champion of lost causes, an organiser, letter writer and litigant on behalf of his illiterate neighbours.

As my father systematically went through the contents of the bureau, he learned a great deal that was new to him—the Suters were not a very communicative family—but threw nothing away, in case it was important. How often have I had cause to be grateful to him for his inherited instinct to hoard!

Many years later, when both my parents were dead and the bureau was mine, I discovered the greatest treasure of all. Inside a tin that had once held *Andies Candies*, I found seven faded letters which revealed the life story of a remarkable woman—my great-great aunt, Ellen Read, née Suter.

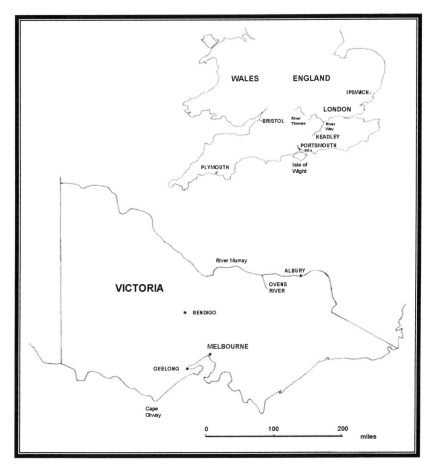

Southern England and the State of Victoria drawn to the same scale

The Suters of Portsea

❧ ❧ ❧

*Before we turn to the letters, let me set the scene
and give a background to Ellen's early life.*

My then 32-year-old great-great-grandfather William Suter and his
already-pregnant 19-year-old bride Frances Chiverton were married
at St Mary's, Portsea in 1815. He was a shipwright, but it was a
period when the fortunes of the area were at a very low ebb. War was
a prosperous time for naval shipyards, and the end of the Napoleonic
Wars had brought them great distress. Low wages and
unemployment meant a full poorhouse, and hundreds of paupers
outside it.

The Suters' first home was in Marlborough Row, a one-sided
street facing the dockyard wall and ending in one of the gates to the
yard. Here their first child, Amelia, was born, but she only lived nine
months, by which time they were living in Unicorn Street.

Their second child, my great-grandfather William, was born in
Britain Street in 1817, but by 1819 when their third child Emma was
born, they had been reduced to moving to Pollard Court, a very low
area indeed, with only one privy shared by all the shoddily-built
houses and an open ditch running across it. Emma, it seems, did not
live long.

The next move was back to Gloucester Street, east of and parallel
to Marlborough Row. It was here that Helen (Ellen), their fourth
child, was born on 23rd February 1822.

It was also where they were living when, in May 1827, William
the elder died. Frances, pregnant again, was left a widow — and in
June she bore twins, Edwin and Emma Ann.

Edwin died the following year aged sixteen months, and Frances,
aged 32, was left with three children to care for: William aged 10,
Helen (Ellen) 5, and baby Emma Ann.

How did the family manage? William was probably old enough
to earn some money. There are two oral traditions in our family from

this time: one mentions an association with Vicat Cole, the landscape painter; the other says that William lived in Penny Street, which is where Vicat Cole lived.

I have often wondered how William, the son of a shipwright, became a paper-maker when there were no paper mills near his childhood home. Did he go to work for Vicat Cole, who guided him into a career less unpredictable than shipbuilding? It is unfortunate that there are so few sources of information about this period of the Suter family's history. But we do know that the members went their separate ways to escape from the poverty of Portsea.

By the time of the first detailed National Census of June 1841, Frances 'Fanny' Suter, aged 46, was a nurse in the household of William Chiverton, I assume a relation, perhaps brother, at Carisbrooke in the Isle of Wight; William her son, aged 24, was a papermaker at Standford, a hamlet on the southern River Wey at Headley, Hampshire; Emma Ann, aged 14, was presumably in service (we have not discovered where yet) — and Ellen, aged 19, was on the high seas, just forty-three days away from landing in Australia and beginning a new life for herself.

Flight from Poverty

ᘰᘯᘰᘯᘰᘯ

Ellen Suter, house-servant aged 19, and Fanny Rose, bonnet-maker aged 24, are the only two emigrants listed as being from Portsmouth among the passengers on the ship *Westminster*, which arrived at Port Phillip on July 30th 1841.

It had taken 104 days to reach Australia, having sailed from Plymouth on April 17th. What led these two young women to embark on so hazardous a journey to a new life on the other side of the world, with very little prospect of ever seeing home or family again? From Ellen's letters we can infer that it was despair at conditions in Portsea. Probably she had had to work as a servant from the age of ten or eleven, but at least she had learned to read and write. The Beneficial and Social School (built in 1785) was nearby.

She would have seen the sailing ships moving in and out of the Solent and heard the adults talking about the opportunities in the new colonies. Perhaps eventually she read a poster advertising the Bounty for young people, particularly females, who were urgently needed in Australia.

The British Government was only too glad to reduce the population, especially to get rid of the very poor, so it willingly provided rations and bedding on the emigrant ships, packing as many as possible into the space available in steerage. Having made up her mind to go—since nothing could be worse, even the unknown must be better—Ellen had to prepare for the journey. I imagine she had few possessions to pack, but she would have been warned that certain provisions were essential: raspberry vinegar and ginger to disguise the brackish drinking water taken from the rivers at ports of call; sewing materials, soap (although she would have to wash in salt water) and any other equipment such as bedding that she would need in the new country.

What to pack? Apart from a working dress and apron, most women would have possessed only two dresses, one for winter, another for summer. On the ship, apart from the hooks above their bunks there was nowhere to store clothes, so their bulky dresses and voluminous underclothes had to be worn for a month at a time. Then on a fine day the heavy luggage was brought up from the hold and unpacked for airing and a change of clothes.

The *Westminster* left Gravesend on April 4th and Plymouth on April 17th 1841, but there is no record of her having called at Portsmouth on the way, so we do not know where Ellen and Rose embarked. The usual custom was to herd Bounty emigrants together like cattle in a depot shed to await the arrival of the ship, which could not accurately be calculated as sail was so dependent on the weather.

On board they were once more herded together below decks in a compartment the length of the vessel; single men at one end, families in the middle and single women at the other end with partitions to separate them. It was dark and cramped, and measured 6ft 4ins from the floor to the deck above.

A long table in the middle stretched the length of the space, with fixed bench seats on either side, and underneath storage space for cooking utensils, crockery and water casks. Around the walls were the sleeping areas, two tiers of wooden shelves divided into spaces 6ft long and 3ft wide with 2ft 11ins between upper and lower bunks. Hooks at the head of each bunk held clothes, and single women had to sleep two to a bed.

How could they bear to spend over three months in these conditions with no privacy? But then most of them had been living in equally poor accommodation at home. Here there was no escape from the heat, the noise, the smells: sea-sickness, chamber-pots, unwashed bodies, musty clothing, oil lamps, lingering reminders of past cargoes in the hold. In good weather they could enjoy the relief of exercise on deck, but in bad weather the hatches were closed and even then they were sometimes swamped with sea-water.

Perhaps the strangest part of shipboard life was the endless leisure. They had all been used to hard work from sunrise to sunset so that any spare moments had been precious. At sea they had very little to do, so at first a great deal of the time was spent in talking, getting to know each other and wondering about, and planning, their new life. Those who were literate were encouraged to keep journals or to help others to learn to read; they played board games and enjoyed sing-songs.

It is so difficult for us to imagine what life was like before electronic communication. The journey to Australia was in effect three months in limbo, out of touch with the world except for ports of call unless a passing ship happened to be within hailing distance—this actually was the case with the *Westminster* when, on May 14th, the *Wave* spoke to her.

The usual route was to the Cape Verde Islands, Rio, and Cape Town, which was the last sight of land until Cape Otway. The second half of the voyage was the worst, and must have seemed interminable. By now, although some firm friendships had been established, many of the passengers were getting on each other's nerves, and tempers became frayed. Bad weather, too, was more frequent. Ellen probably wrote letters or kept a journal. If so I wonder whether it still exists somewhere? Perhaps with some of her descendants?

At last the long journey was over, and from Cape Otway up to Port Phillip surely her spirits would rise, for the prospect was really beautiful. The 246 passengers had arrived in good health, and the Immigration Agent received £4,192 for his "cargo" safely delivered.

But it was a difficult time for the authorities. One thousand five hundred immigrants had arrived in one week, so there was not enough employment to go round, wages fell and 500 people had to be lodged in temporary tented accommodation in Melbourne. The city was still at the planning stage, and the so-called streets nothing but lanes in which were stagnant pools, mud, filth, and rubbish.

Many of their fellow passengers had dispersed to join relatives or take up prearranged employment, but Ellen was simply listed as having 'left the ship' in Melbourne for £15 wages with rations. The last link with home had been broken, and in discomfort and despair they faced an uncertain future. However uncomfortable the conditions on board, they had enjoyed security, with beds, food and medical attention better than they would have had at home.

All Saints' Church, Headley c.1843

Meanwhile, in England

'Fanny' Suter must have followed her son William to Standford soon after Ellen had left for Australia, for in February 1843 we find her marrying Joseph Howard, a widower and papermaker of Standford at All Saints' Church, Headley. His wife had died in June the previous year. Their marriage did not last long however, as Joseph died six months later, and is buried in Headley churchyard with his first wife.

The next we hear of Fanny is in March 1848, when she is living in Sackville Street, Southsea, and marrying her third husband, William Barnett of Headley at the Ebenezer Baptist Chapel in Portsea. But in the census of March 1851, they are back living in the parish of Headley again, in Arford: William an agricultural labourer aged 57, and she aged 58.

By this time, both her daughter Emma and her son William are married: Emma of King St, Southsea in 1847 to Charles Rishman Baker; and William in 1848 to Eliza Chiverton of Carisbrooke, Isle of Wight, who we assume from her surname and location was a relative of Fanny's family.

In fact, all Fanny's children were now married as, unknown to her, Ellen had married in Melbourne at the age of 20 and was by now a mother several times over — but that is a story for the next chapter.

We assume that Fanny lived in Headley for the rest of her life. She died in April 1863 aged 67, and is buried in Headley churchyard. William Barnett outlived her by eight years.

In view of all these changes of address and surname, is it any wonder that poor Ellen, half a world away in Australia, lost touch with her mother and siblings?

St James Cathedral, Melbourne c.1843

To the Gold Diggings

Ellen Suter married James Read of Ipswich at St James Cathedral, Melbourne on 17th January 1843. He was 43 and described as a bachelor of Ovens River, NSW; she was just one month short of her 21st birthday and described as a spinster 'of this parish'.

Their first child to survive, William James, was born to them in 1845, when they were living in the Goulburn/Ovens River area on the Victoria/NSW border. Other children arrived in succession: Frances Emma (also called Fanny) was born in 1847, then Elizabeth Susan (1848), John Suter (1850), George Edwin (c.1853), Walter John (1855), twins Arthur Benjamin and Ada Louise (1857), twins James and Alice Ellen (1860), and finally twins Rosetta (Rose) and Lilian in 1862.

They had moved to Eaglehawk near Bendigo in Victoria by 1853, the date of the first letter which has survived from her. This was the year after the first gold nugget had been found there.

Since the day she had arrived in Australia, Ellen tells us that she had been sending letters back to England, but had received only one reply in twelve years.

Suddenly in 1853, after a flurry of writing fifteen letters in twelve months, it appears that she began to get answers from her brother William in Headley.

The SS *Great Britain*, launched in 1843,
had started to make voyages to Australia in 1852
which speeded up the transfer of mail considerably.

The Letters

❧ ❧ ❧

Written on wafer-thin blue paper, folded, creased and faded, the first letter was in places difficult to decipher, but the very first sentence alone spoke to me over a gap of more than one hundred years.

"My Dear Sister, Weary is the task to me to address another letter to you, for so hopeless seems the prospect of my receiving any answer."

Who was this woman crying out in despair from the other side of the world to her unnamed sister?

"I have written now 15 letters this last twelve month to you, Mother and William...."

Why had no-one answered her letters? It was certainly not because they were illiterate, so had she been disowned by her family when she decided to emigrate?

It has taken me thirty years to find the answers to some of these questions, and the more I discovered, the more questions arose.

One thing became very clear as I read the rest of the letters. Ellen Read was an excellent communicator, with a natural turn of phrase to express her emotions and to describe her family and the way of life, which differed so much from her early years in England.

Shaky spelling and lack of punctuation are only minor hindrances that do very little to disturb the flow of feeling and the sense of a strong personality that remains alive in these words written so long ago.

Note: In transcripts, numbers eg [2] show the start of original pages.

Bendigo Gold
Diggins July 29/53

My Dear Sister

Weary is the task to me
to address another letter to you for
so hopeless seem the prospect of my
receiving any answer. twelve years ago
the 29 of this month and only one letter
have I received from any of you to
remind me of Mother Brothers Sister
and friend, uncle, once my home, at
though so long here still my thoughts
often wander to you, wondering how
you are passing on this struggling
world, I am sure your prospects
are not over bright. which makes
me dubly anxious to hear from you
I have written now. 15 letters this last
twelve month to you mother and Wo ...
if you have received any of them
I need not mention the age on the
picture gold fields how I wish you
where hear, how many a new hund
in the Colony have I seen raised from
poverty by immence riches in one
day, indeed when first the Gold was
found many have obtained two hundred
weigh of Gold in one lumps, many
have done well, only to indulge in
drunkness and vice but many have
done well to benefit others, we have
not be one of the most fortunate
Class but still have done well

First letter — 20th July 1853

Bendigo Gold Diggins, July 20/53
My Dear Sister
Weary is the task to me to address another letter to you, for so hopeless seem the prospect of my receving any answer. Twelve years ago the 29 of this month, and only one letter have I receved from any of you to remind me of Mother, Brothers, Sister and friend, and once my home. Although so long here, still my thoughts often wander to you, wondering how you are faring in this strugling world. I am sure your prospects are not over bright, which makes me dubly anxous to hear from you.

I have writen now 15 letters this last twelve month to you, Mother and William. If you have recieved any of them, I need not mention we are on the Victoria gold fields. How I wish you where hear. How many a new hand in the Colony have I seen raised from poverty to immence riches in one day, indeed when first the gold was found many have obtained two hundred weigh of gold in one lump. Many have done well only to indulge in drunkeness and vice, but many have done well to benifit others. We have not be one of the most fortunate class, but still have done well.

[2] I have writen to William to know if he has any wish to come out, and also to you, but if you have any ~~wish~~ objection, for of course you know your own wants better than me.

I will send three hundred pound between Mother, William and you to help you on a little, only be sure and write so that I may know your abode. I have sent money to Mother twice, and not receving any answer of the delivery of the same makes me more careful for the future. The way that I sent it was in Bill of Exchange from the Bank of Australia on the Bank of England. One was sent in 49 for the sum of 40 pounds, the last in January 52 for the same amount. Let me know weather it was recieved, as of course I must apply to the Bank here for the amount if not duly delivered, but we have [thirty] pound weight of gold we [...] home to London for sale which will be shiped in the Great Britain steamer which is hourly expected. We shall have to get a agent in London, which will be the best way to send to you. I have one favour to ask of you, which is to send me sometimes the times Newspaper and the Ilustrated London News. Any thing connected with home has a charm.

I have written to William to know
he has any wish to come out and
do to you, but if you have any
objection for of course you know
your own wants better than me I will
send three hundred pound between Mother
William and you to help you on a little
only be sure and write so that I may
know your abode I have sent money
to Mother twice and not receiving any
answer of the delivery of the same
makes me more careful for the future
the way that I sent it was a bill
of exchange from the Bank of Australia
on the Bank of England one was sent
in 49 for the sum of 40 pounds the loss
in January 52 for the same amount
let me know weather it was received
of course I must apply to the Bank
here for the amount if not duly delivered
but we have it pounds weight of
gold we are going home to London for
sale which will be shiped in the Great
Britain steamer which is hourly expected
we shall have to get a agent in London
which will be the best way to send to
you, I have one favour to ask of
you which is to send me sometimes
the times Newspaper and the Illustrated
London News any thing connected with
home has a Charm.. I expect by this
time you have quite a family near I
have only one. the three eldest being
in Melbourn at school but in one
more month will be with them

I expect by this time you have quite a family. Hear I have only one, the three eldest being in Melbourn at school, but in one more month will be with them [3] for I am very unhappy without them. William my eldest boy is just eight year old and is getting on very fast, Fanny is seven years old, a curly head fat girl very strong but bids fare to be a very promising, she has just began to learn the piano. Elizabeth is five years next month, a little tiny thing but a general favourate and pronounced to be the flower of the flock. She has made no progress as yet in learning. John Suter is three years, my younges alive and the greatest rogue. We never can find it in our heart to correct him for he will coaxe us out of every thing. He often says he will grow a big man and dig a big hole and get gold, to send home to his Uncle in England. He is a very strong boy and bids fare to be the sort that wanted for digging holes.

If William have recived any of my letters you will know the way we get on digging for gold, but it is a lottery, many blank, but by persevering you may get a great prise a always a good living. But still trade of all kind is flourishing fast and things very high. Washing we have to pay from twelve shillings per dozen for, so that gold need be plentyful, as potatoe and onions, from where I now write, is two shillings per pound, a small sprout of cabbage three shillings. That gardening pays well [4] as gold digging. I cannot say much more until I have an answer from some of you. I have written to Mother and William, but give my kindest love to them and accept the same for you

Ellen A Suter

[...] to remember us to all relations and friends [...]

Mrs James E Read
Post Office
Melbourn
Colony of Victoria
Australia

for I am very unhappy without them William
my eldest boy is just eight years old and
is getting on very fast Fanny is seven years
old a curly head fat girl very strong but
bids fair to be a very promising she
has just begun to learn the piano
Elizabeth is five years next month a little
tiny thing but a general favourite and pro
nounced to be the flower of the flock, she
has made no progress as yet in learning
John Suter is three years my youngest alive
and the greatest rogue we never can
find it in our hearts to correct him for
he will coaxe us out of every thing, he often
says he will grow a big man and
dig a big hole and get gold, to send
home to his Uncle in England, he is a
very strong boy and bids fair, be the
sort that wanted for diggers holes
if William have received any of my letters
you will know the way we get on dig
for gold but it is all a lottery many
blanks, but by by persevering you may
get a great prize to always a good
lives but still trade of all kind
is flourishing fast and things very
high, washing we have to pay two
twelve shillings her dozen for that
that Gold need be plentyful
as potatoe and onions from where
I now write is two shillings per pound
a small sprout of cabbage three
shillings that Gardening pays well

Notes to First Letter, 20th July 1853:

The date of her arrival in Australia in 1841 is obviously very firmly imprinted on Ellen's mind. We assume that she was writing this letter to her younger sister Emma Ann, but it must have been passed on to her brother William for us to have found it among the others.

In July 1853, Ellen Read was 31 years old, had been married for ten years to a man much older than herself, and had given birth to seven children, two having died unnamed—presumably still-born. Despite our being told he is a 'strong boy,' John Suter Read was to die relatively young.

She mentions having written previously to 'mother, brothers, sister and friend,' but we know of only one brother living at the time, William. Her younger brother Edwin had died in infancy before she left England. I wonder, was this simply a spelling mistake, or was there another brother whom we are not aware of?

Ellen had evidently prospered materially, and was anxious to help her family living, as she remembered, in very straitened circumstances. The three hundred pounds which she is sending to them was in those days a considerable sum of money—equivalent perhaps to about £5,000 at the end of the 20th century.

She asks for confirmation of where her sister lives, evidently suspecting that the family must have moved and that this was why she had received neither letter nor even acknowledgement of the two Bills of Exchange for £40. Yet still she wrote to the old addresses, "fifteen letters this last twelve month." It is difficult to imagine having the persistence to write five letters a year each to mother, brother and sister with not a word in reply.

Often it is a small detail that causes most surprise. Given her impoverished background and her subsequent life on the gold fields, who would have expected Ellen to ask her sister to send her *The Times* ("the Top Peoples' Newspaper") and *The Illustrated London News*!

Note: Final page facsimile not shown as it is too feint

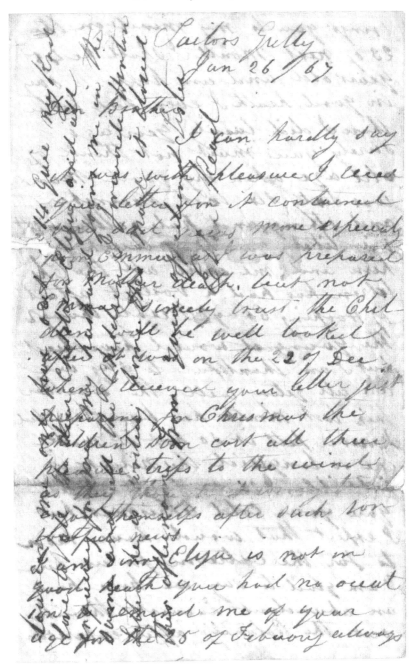

Second letter — 26th January 1867

Sailors Gully, Jan 26/67
Dear Brother

I can hardly say it was with pleasure I read your letter for it contained very sad news, more especialy poor Emma as I was prepared for Mother death, but not Emma. I sincerely trust the children will be well looked after. It was on the 22 of Dec when I recieved your letter, just preparing for Christmas. The children soon cast all thier pleasure trips to the wind as they thought it was wrong to enjoy themselfs after such sorrowful news.

I am sorry Eliza is not in good health. You had no occation to remind me of your age, for the 25 of February always [2] brings you to my mind. On the 23 of next month I shall be 45 years old and am happy to say in good health. I even feel better than I did twenty year ago. Surely you must not think of old age when my good man was sixty six last November and strong and hale, although very likely you may laugh, for him and me and all the children has had a voilent attact of Hooping Cough. I realy thought the youngest would have died, but I am thankful to say we are all geting well. The weather this last month has been dreadful, I never felt it so hot. It made one so languid the night, is intorible. I realy begrudged you your cold Chrismas, but I expect that woud have been to far the extreem for us here. I am glad to say we have had an abundant harvest throuh out the Colony, after experison [3] two years of drough which brough things to famine price. Thier was not feed for the cattle and meat was very dear. For my family the Beef we would use in one week would amount to £1.10. As people here cannot do without a large quanty for animal food, at present Beef and Mutton is 3 pence per pound, flour £1.8 per bag of two hundred weight, vegatable and fruit in abundance.

Respecting ourselves, we have no cause to complain. We have taken a large contract for the Catherine Crushing Engine. They consume 100 tons of wood weakly. Thier yeald of gold has been enormous, still for all that they have not yet declared a dividend. We hold 200 shares which I hope will soon realize some return. We have also 200 in the Star Company which at present looks very bad; we have to pay into it 6 pence per share monthly.

31

brings you to my mind on the
23 of next month I shall be 45
years old and am happy to say
in good health I even feel better
than I did twenty year ago
surely you must not think of
old age when my good man
was sixty six last November
and strong and hale although
very likely you may laugh of
him and me all the Chil
dren has had a violent attack
of Hooping Cough I truly though
the youngest would have died
but I am thankful to say we
are all getting well, the weather
this last month has been dreadful
I never felt it so hot it make
one so languid the night is
intolerable I could have wished
you your cold Christmas but
I expect that would have been
to far the extreme for us here
I am glad to say we have had
an abundant harvest through
out the Colony after experience

[4] *I have forwarded you two likeness. One is my daughter Fanny and her husband; they where takeing before her marrig. I have not seen her since the morning they wher married as they live 200 miles from here. They where well when I last heard from them.*

Elizabeth send her kind love to all her Cousins. She is 18 years old and does all my house work. I think she will be a old maid. She is a very proud girl. Next mail she will send her likeness and a present to her cousin Fanny.

My two boy are well and hard at work. You must find your boys great use to you now.

Our pet Rosa says she wants to see her cousin Edith. She is four years old and the last of six, as I had twins 3 time running. All has died but her; although every care and attention was given them, they all went. Ada the oldest of the six died at five years old. This is a dreadful country for children you must know. I have had my trouble loosing so many children, [cross-writing on Page 1] *leaving me only five out of 14. Give my kind love to all the dear Children, Eliza and all enquiring for me. My husband joins me in the same, and all the children. I forward Hinton letter he is writing home this mail; it closed this afternoon.*

Your affectionat Sister
Ellen Read

these years of drought which forced things to famine price there was not feed for the Cattle and Meat was very dear for my family the Beef we would use in one week would amount to £1.10 - as people here cannot do without a large quanty of Animal food at present Beef and Mutton; hence we found Flour £1-8 per Bag of two hundred weight vegatable and fruit in abundance

respecting ourselves we have no cause to complain we have taken a large Contract for the Catherine Crushing Engine they consume 100 tons of wood weekly there yeald of gold has been enormous still for all that they have not yet declared a dividend, we hold 200 shares which I hope will soon realise some return we have also 200 in the Star Company which at present looks very bad we have to pay into it 6 pence per share monthly

Notes to Second Letter, 26th January 1867:

Evidently, William kept only the letters of special significance since there is a gap of thirteen years between the first and second that have survived. This one is especially valuable to a genealogist because it contains so many dates and facts which can be verified.

Back home in England her mother had died nearly 4 years ago—she had been buried in Headley churchyard in April 1863—yet here Ellen speaks of it as if it were a recent event.

Ellen had had two sisters named Emma, quite a usual custom in those days when the first died young. The one mentioned here must have been the youngest of the family, Emma Ann, who married Charles Richman Baker in 1846, but whose children and death I have not been able to trace as yet.

William would be 50 on the 25th February 1867. By this time he had his complete family: George (born 1852), William (1855), and Edith (1859), and was living at Standford in Headley parish. In view of the gaps between their ages, and the small size of the family for those days, I wonder whether Eliza's poor health was due to several miscarriages, or whether she had TB or some other chronic illness brought on by her work in the paper-mill. In the 1861 census she is described as a 'Paper Bag Maker' while he is a 'Papermaker Foreman.'

Ellen gives us further facts and figures of interest to historians.

James Read was not a miner. He is described as a wood-splitter, and with his two sons provided the wood for the fires which drove the Catherine engine. This crushed the quartz ore so that the gold could be extracted.

Did the family's shares in the Star Company ever pay a dividend? If not, £5 a month was hardly a profitable outlay.

By this time Ellen also had her complete family. Out of fourteen births the only survivors when this letter was written were William, Fanny, Elizabeth, Walter and Rose.

We do not know who Hinton was. He is mentioned several times in the letters, and Ellen writes as if her brother William was acquainted with him. Is there someone reading this who can tell me?

See the 'likeness' of Fanny and her husband Charles Cook
on the following page.

I have forwarde you two like
ness one is my daughter Fanny
and her husband they where take
ing before her morning I have
not seen her since the morning
they where married as they live
200 miles from here they where well
when I last heard from them
Elizabeth send her kind love to
all her Cousins. She is 18 years old
and does all my house work I think
she will be a old maid she is
a very proud girl next must she
will send her likeness and a
present to her Cousin Fanny
My two boy are well and hard
at work you must find your boys
great use to you now
Our pet Rosa sayes she wants
to see her Cousin Edith she is four
years old and the last of six as
I had twins 3 times and all has
died but her although every Care and
attention was given them they all
went Ada the oldest of the six
died at five years old this is a
dreadful Country for Children
you must know I have had my
trouble loosing so many Children

Frances (Fanny) Read and Charles Cook before their marriage 1866

Paitors Gully
September 26/67

Dear Brother
It was with feelings of great pleasure I received your last letter and was happy that Eliza is better & your dear Children was well If I could only see you once more is the wish of my life one hardly knows what may happen in a Country full of Changes if I had gone to England 12 years ago how different we should have been but I do not repine my destiny must be fulfilled at the present time we are under a cloud as Elizabeth went to Melbourne in January last to pass an examina tion as a Teacher for the National School Eaglehawk she was down three months and obtained a second Class Certificate which will entitle her to £60 pound per year she had only commenced her duty when she took ill with Colonial fever the doctor only last week pronounced her out of danger I sincerely trust it may last you must excuse me from writing

Third letter — 26th September 1867

Sailors Gully, September 26/67

Dear Brother

It was with feelings of great pleasure I recieved your last letter, and was happy that Eliza is better, also your dear children was well. If I could only see you once more, is the aim of my life. One hardly knows what may happen in a country full of changes. If I had gone to England 12 years ago how different we should have been, but I do not repine; my destiny must be fulfilled. At the present time we are under a cloud, as Elizabeth went to Melbourn in January last to pass an examination as a Teacher for the National School, Eaglehawk. She was down three months and obtained a second class Certificat which will entitle her to £60 pound per year. She had only commenced her duty when she took ill with Colonial fever. The doctor only last week pronounced her out of danger; I sincerly trust it may last. You must excuse me from writing [2] before on account of her illness, also of her writing to her cousin Fanny.

I sent you a paper in May last announcing the birth of Fanny baby which was born at Eaglehawk on the 19 of May. She came down from the Murray to her mother in laws to be confined. You may depend it has been quite an event. The dear babe has been baptized Emma Ada, but I am sorry her breast took bad and was not able to suckel the baby, but she was able to secure the service of a wet nurse at one pound per week which is gone to the Murray with her two month ago. By last advices the child was doing well. You did her great injustice respecting the likeness, for thier is not a better tempered girl anywhere. She is greatly esteemed for her general good temper. Also her husband is a native of the Colony, the same as herself, his father being an Englishman his Mother Scotch. He is the eldest of a large family. She is, I am happy to say, very comfortable. The [3] marriage has turned out better than Read expected; he was greatly against it at first.

Rose is so pleased with Edith for sending the picture. We had a great deal of trouble with her of a night saying her prayers; she would pray for Cousin Edith before Fanny's baby. She do not like the dear babe, but the truth it is jealousy. By the way, how did you find such a pretty name for your little girl?

before on account of her illness
also of her writing to her Cousin
Fanny

I sent you a paper in May last
announcing the birth of Fanny baby
which was born at Eaglehawk on
the 19 of May she came down from
the Murray to her Mother in Laws
to be confined you may depend
it has been quite an Event the
dear babe has been baptized, Emma
Ada but I am sorry her breast
broke bad and was not able to suck
it the baby but she was able to
secure the service of a wet nurse
at one pound her week which is
gone to the Murray with her two
month ago by last advices the
child was doing well you did her
great injustice respecting the likeness
for there is not a better tempered
girl anywhere she is greatly esteem
ed for her general good temper
also her husband is a native
of the Colony the same as herself
his father being an Englishman his
mother Scotch he is the eldest of
a large family she is I am happy
to say very comfortable the marriage

40

Walter wishes he could be in England only to see snow. He has no idea what it is like, but the only consolation he has that he can pick up gold after the rain which must be better than snow balls – he has forwarded a sample to his cousins what he pick up after rain.

I am very sorry George is fond of rambling, for he is too young to meet the hardships of Australian life. Tell him he would be astonished at the privation many has to endure at the digings with very little [4] profit. My boys when after timber or game will go out and sleep in the bush miles from the habitation of man without even a blanket. Boys reared in England would never thing of. To bring a trade may do very well if gold failed. I should like to see your boys; I could give them many accounts of Australian life that has come under my own notice.

Emma likeness would be the greatest boon. You could send also accounts of the dear children. Be sure and let me know.

You sent Uncle William likeness; you never told me was he dead or alive. I often think of him; to tell the truth I seem to think more of him than any of our relatives. How is Cousin Ellen and, I must refresh your memorie, all of Uncle Roberts Hinton has a letter by last mail from his sister. She seems to have a poor account of us from being in the diggins. She has heard it is no better than a hell on [5] Earth. I can assure you it is a great lible. I have been on the diggings in its infancy and never saw anything immorrall, nor me or mine been molested in any shape or form. Where we live is in a Gully worked out. No one living nere, still we can sleep without a lock on our door. It is true what money we have we bank so thier is no temtation. We live two miles from Eaglehawk township. Still it has as many places of worship as public houses. Thier Church of England, Baptist, Bible Christians, Methodist, Wesleyans, Presbyterians and draws large congregation. I have brough up all my children to the Church of England; I go no were else myself.

My boys are quite well and still going on with thier contract which is nearly done. The Catherine Reef is doing very well but no yet declared a divident.

You may depend the Colony [6] is quite mad respecting the arrival of Prince Alfred. He his not expected here till next month, when I expect all homage will be done to him. I would not miss the opportunity of seeing him on any a/c.

41

Marriage has turned out better than
Read expected he was greatly again
st it at first

Rose is so pleased with Edith
for sending the picture we had a
great deal of trouble with her
of a night saying her prayers she
would pray for Cousin Edith he
fine Fanny baby she do not like
the dear babe but the truth is
is jealousy, by the way how did
you find such a pretty mame
for your little girl,

Walter wishes he could be in England only to see I now he has
no idea what it is like but the
only consolation he has that he
can pick up gold after the rain
which must be better than Snow
balls - he has forwarded a sample
to his Cousins what he pick up
after rain

I am very sorry George is fond of
rambling for he is too young to
meet the hardships of Australian
life till him he would be astonished
at the privateen many has to endure
at the diggings with very little

42

Our winter has been very wet but very warm. The crop is looking beautiful. Every thing is very cheap; meat is reducing in price every day, as low as two pence per pound for mutton, beef three pence. It is a great change from our former prices.

I hope you will write to us soon and let me know how you all are, and if you could put a few seed of primroses and forget me not in the letter, I have English voilets growing beautiful in the garden. Accept the kindnes love of us all and belive me to be your affectionat Sister Ellen Read

PS not forgetting my kindest love to Eliza and the children

profit my boys when after timber
or game will go out and sleep
in the bush miles from the habit
ation of Man without even a Blan
ket boys reared in England would
never thing of, to bring a trade may
do very well if gold failed I should
like to see your boys I could give
them many accounts of Australian
life that has come under my
own notice

Emma likeness would be the great
est boon you could send also ac
counts of the dear Children be sure
and let me know

You sent Uncle William likeness you
never told me was he dead or
alive I often think of him to tell
the truth I seem to think more of
him than any of our relatives
how is Cousin Ellen and I must
refresh your memorie all of Uncle
Roberts Children
Hinton has a letter by last Mail from
from his Sister she seem to have a
poor account of us from being
in the diggins she has heard
it is no better than a hell on

Notes to Third Letter, 26th September 1867:

It is interesting to note that she had thought of returning to England in 1855 when she already had four children and twins were born that year. Just a visit? Unlikely in those days. A difficult phase in the marriage? Or hard times, and the possibility that conditions would be better back home?

Elizabeth, her third surviving child and "flower of the flock" was now nineteen. I have been given various theories concerning what was meant by Colonial Fever. It may have been a summer infection caused by poor sanitation, or atmospheric pollution and impure water; a form of dysentery, gastro-enteritis or malaria.

We assume that Elizabeth's 'cousin Fanny' was a daughter of Ellen's sister Emma Ann whose death was reported in the previous letter.

The Fanny in the next paragraph is Ellen's eldest daughter, born in 1846 and married to Charles Cook in the new St Peter's Anglican Church at Eaglehawk on June 4th 1866. Although they were living 'over 200 miles away' on the Murray in NSW, Fanny returned to Eaglehawk for her first confinement — though not in her parents' house, but with her mother-in-law. Emma Ada was born on 19th May 1867.

By one of those wonderful strokes of good luck—coincidence or serendipity?—so helpful to all genealogists, Gaye Dwyer of Victoria, was researching her Cook family history, heard of me, and sent me invaluable information about them. As she herself says, no wonder that James Read was initially against the marriage. Charles' father had been transported from England for stealing oats, and his conduct was described as "bad to indifferent". He seems to have been a thoroughly awkward customer for the rest of his life, truculent and dishonest, and eventually died in an asylum. Fanny's husband was of a different calibre, and is recorded as a miner and overseer. His mother, too, a Scot who went out as an assisted emigrant, was evidently a great support to the young wife.

Once again I marvel at Ellen Read's skill at conveying strong family feeling in a few simple words. How typically tactless of an older brother to make derogatory remarks about his niece's looks; and how like a five-year-old to have her nose put out of joint by the arrival of her sister's baby. We can still sympathise with these feelings more than a century later, for people's emotions haven't changed.

Earth I can assure you it is a great
little I have been on the diggings in
its infancy and never saw any
thing immoral, nor me or mine
been molested in any shape or
form where we live is in a gully
worked out no one living near
still we can sleep without a lock
on our door, it is true what more
we have the Bank so there is
no temtation, we live two miles
from Eaglehawk township still
it has as many pates of worship
as public houses their Church of
England, Babtist Bible Christian
Methodist Wesleyan, Presbytrian
and draws large congregation,
I have brought up all my Children
to the Church of England I go
no were else myself

My boys are quite well and
still going on with their Contract
which is nearly done. the Catherine
Reef is doing very well but not
yet declared a dividend —
You may depend the Colony

Walter, now aged twelve, consoles himself for lack of snow by the thought that English George can't pick up gold after the rain has uncovered it. I wonder what happened to the samples they forwarded? Perhaps turned into a trinket, or set in a watch-chain? I have never found them, not even in the old bureau.

George at this time was five years old. When an adult, the furthest that he 'rambled' was to Manchester where he did indeed continue to work in a mill, but in the cotton industry which required many of the same skills as papermaking. Somewhat different from the 'hardships of Australian life'.

Unfortunately we have not found a picture of Emma Ann, though from this letter I assume that one must have existed. We also gather from this that more than one child survived her.

Uncles William and Robert and Cousin Ellen were relatives on the Chiverton side.

This is not the first time that Ellen has alluded to the low opinion of those in Britain towards life at the gold diggings, and jumped to the defence of the Australians.

Eaglehawk township had by this time grown in fifteen years since gold was first found to be a sizeable town of over 20,000 inhabitants.

Prince Alfred, Duke of Edinburgh, was Queen Victoria's second son and figures prominently in the following letters—not always to his advantage.

I wonder if the primrose and forget-me-not seeds arrived from Headley, and if so whether they and the violets are still flowering in Sailor's Gully?

quite mad respecting the arrival
of Prince Alfred he has not arrived
here till next month when I expect
all homage will be done to him
I would not miss the opportunity
of seeing him on any a/c

our winter has been very wet
but very warm the Crops is looking
beautiful every thing is very
Cheap Meat is reducing in price
every day as low as two pence
her pound for Mutton, Beef
three pence it is a great change
from our former prices

I hope you will write to us soon
and let me know how you all
are and if you could put a
line out of numerous and
forget me not in the letter I have
English Violets growing beautiful
in the garden, accept the Kindest
love of us all and believe me
to be your affectionate Sister

       Ellen Read

P.S. not forgetting my Kindest love
to Eliza and the Children

William Read, Ellen's eldest child, aged about 30

Eagle hawk Sep 10
1868

Dear Brother

I did not receive your
letter of Febuary untill July do not
send any more letters by the Panama
route as they all go to Sydney and
is charged to the victorean double
postage I was very happy to hear
of your all been well and comfortable
and your Children provided for
better then you when a boy they
can not know all the hardships
you had to contend with I would
not like to be poor with a family
in England, for here you may
have a chance of bettering one
self since I last wrote to you
we have received your Prince
and sent him home that it
was a cowardly act my Children
is so glad it did not occur in
victoria for there is a jealousy
between the different colonys the
man was hung for the offence

50

Fourth letter — 10th September 1868

Eaglehawk, Sep 10 1868
Dear Brother
I did not receive your letter of February until July. Do not send any more letters by the Panama route as they all go to Sydney and is charged to the Victorians double postage. I was very happy to hear of your all been well and comfortable, and your Children provided for better than you when a boy. They can not know all the hardships you had to contend with. I would not like to be poor with a family in England, for hear you may have a chance of bettering one self.

Since I last wrote to you we have recieved your Prince and sent him home shot. It was a cowardly act. My children is so glad it did not occur in Victoria, for thier is jealousy between the different Colonys. The man was hung for the offence.

[2] The indignation of the people was extreem and the Irish was more unpopular than ever. The poor Irish Children could not go to school without being called Fenians. The very children had to show thier feelings in petty squabbles. As it is the Prince was recieved on a grand scale in Bendigo. The torchlight procession of a 1000 miners and illumination was the finest sight I ever witnessed. He also visited the Catherine Engine. As we were share holders we had a ticket of admision, and I had the honor of drinking a glass of Champagne with him. William went to the Banquet, but that was 2 guineas a ticket. Read would not stir out to see him, he saying people was mad to make so much fuss, but as soon as the prince was shot all his loyalty returned. He would not employ any Irish, he would rather do the work himself.

Since I wrote to you Elizabeth has again been very ill, last Chrismas [3] and three months after. I have had the best medical advise and they sayed her right lung was affected, but I am happy to say I think she is perfectly recovered. She is now in Melbourn for the benfit of sea air. As for myself and all the others, are quite well. I heard from Fanny a month ago and she has another daughter. I shall go see her at Chrismas.

the indignation of the people was
esteem and the Irish war more
unpopular than ever the poor Irish
Children could not go to School
without being called Fencing the
very children had to show their
feelings in petty squabbles, as it
is the Prince was received on a
grand scale on Bendigo the torch
light procession of a 1000 miner
and illumination was the finest
sight I ever witnessed he also
visited the Catherine Engine as
we were shareholders we had a
ticket of admission and I had the
honor of Drinking a glass of Champagne with him William went
to the Banquet but that was
2 guineas a ticket. Read would
not stir out to see him he say
ing people was mad to make
so much fuss but as soon as the
prince was shot all his loyalty returned he would not employ
any Irish he would rather do the
work himself.
Since I wrote to you Elizabeth has
again been very ill last Christmas

Things begin to look a little brisker. The Catherine is looking up; the Crushing last fortnight was 300 ounces, the whole of the debt at the bank is payed of, the shares is rising in the market. If they go on this way we shall soon have a return. Thier is also a new gold field opened close to where we live. I have cut a piece from a paper, a description of it for you to see. The great drawback is water. Thier has not been 24 hours rain the whole winter and it is now geting to late for us to expect it. All we can get now is thunder storm as the weather [4] get warm. We live in the Bush 2 miles from the township of Eaglehawk and close to Belzibub gully. The boys has about 50 loads of stuff ready for washing. It may turn out something good. I was wishing to get it washed so I could have sent Edith enough gold to make her something, also poor Emma children. Rose has been looking untill she is tired for some for Edith, thier being no rains to wash the dirt so she could pick it up. The only pieces she had I was compeled to send for quietness. She sets a great prise on what she gets.

I hope all Emma children is well. Let me know how they are all geting, and wish the girls was out hear as it is almost imposible to get a good English servant and they may do well. You may let me know what they thing as I could get them out for a mear trifle, but still if they are in steady places let them be, for if any thing was to happen to them I should regret, for girls is bad property when they are left without the controle of parents. Be sure and write soon and send by the mail direct for Victoria. Give our kindest love to Eliza and the children from your
affection sister

Ellen Read

and three month after I have had
the best medical advice & and they
sayed her right lung was affected
but I am happy to say I think she
is perfully recovered she is now
in Melbourn for the benifit of
sea air. as for myself and all
the others are quite well I heard
from Fanny a month ago and she
has another daughter I shall go
to see her at Chrismas
Things begin to look a little brisk
her the Catherine is looking up
the Chrushing last fortnight was
300 ounces the whole of the debt at
the bank is payed of the shares
is riseing in the market if they
go on this way we shall soon
have a return. there is also a
new gold field opened close to
where we live I have cut a piece
from a paper a descruption of it
for you to see the great drawback
is water there has but been
2½ hours rain the whole winter
and it is now getting to late for
us to expect it all we can get now
is thunder storm as the weather

Notes to Fourth Letter, 10th September 1868:

Another cheerful letter, where, except for Elizabeth's continued poor health, all seems to be going well for both families. I am impressed by Ellen's financial know-how. In those days women were expected to be exclusively concerned with domestic affairs but I think there is no doubt that Ellen was more intelligent (and worldly-wise?) than James, and did all the managing. In fact, perhaps a rather bossy person.

After twenty-seven years she has become an out-and-out colonialist with a strong loyalty to her own colony of Victoria. Note 'your' Prince.

The Read family seemed to enjoy making the most of their import-ance as shareholders in the Catherine Company when Prince Alfred had visited Bendigo in December the previous year. His visit is described from other sources[1] as follows:—

Great demonstrations were made in his honour—nothing so picturesque had been seen as the grouping of the children in one mass on terraces as it were on the hill. At this reception the National Anthem was sung by the children. Altogether there were 6,000 children. They sang in good tune which astonished the Royal visitor.

In the afternoon His Royal Highness visited the Town Hall and in the evening the illuminations were universal throughout the town and the general brilliant effect was heightened by the lurid light thrown from the thousand torches carried by the miners.

Next day the royal party visited a mine where they were shown the plant and the process of crushing. They descended 400 ft to a chamber which was lighted by candles. Champagne was handed around. On reaching the surface the Prince was invited to pick and choose from a case of splendid gold specimens, which he did to a dozen or so.

On 12th March 1868, news was received of the attempted assassination of the Duke in Sydney by a man named O'Farrell, and intense indignation was aroused.

O'Farrell was subsequently hanged, despite claims that he was mentally ill and efforts by the Prince to have his life spared.

---

[1] *Source: Betty Jackman, Bendigo*

get worm we live in the Bush
2 miles from the township of Eaglehawk
and close to Bellibush gully the boys
has about 50 loads of stuff ready for
washing it may turn out something
good I was wishing to get it was
hed so I could have sent Edith in
ugh gold to make her something
also from Emma children Rose has
been looking untill she is tired for
some for Edith their being no rains
to wash the dirt so she could pick
it up, the only heres she had was
compeled to send for quietness she sets
a great prise on what she gets
I hope all Emma children is well let
me know how they are all geting and
wish the girls was out hear as it
is almost imposible to get a good
English servant and they may do
well you may let me know what
they thing as I could get them out
for a mear trifle but still if they are
in steady places let them be for if
any thing was to happen to them I
should regret for girls is bad propely
when they are left without the controle
of parents, be sure and write soon
and send by the mail direct for
pictures give our kindird love to Eliza
and the children from Jane

Ellen heads her letters in various ways; Bendigo Gold Diggings, Sailors Gully or Eaglehawk, but this was an ever-growing community with settlements changing their status.

Betty Jackman gives us a general description of the area:—

Bendigo's topography is in a general way mapped out by its many hills and gullies. These were named by the diggers after some special feature which would identify them. Each had some reference to the name connected with them. Most of the gullies found their way into the Bendigo Creek. Bendigo Creek was one of the biggest of the Australian rushes and its gullies such as Pegleg and Eaglehawk, among the very richest.

Sailor's Gully was the most northerly gully, just outside the township of Eaglehawk.

By this time it was declared a municipality and had a Post Office, but originally it was described as a settlement of poor mining families with a shifting population, as the miners kept moving when new mines opened elsewhere.

June 18/69

Dear Brother

Your last letter came
duly to hand and I should have
answered it before but thinking Mr
Hinton, Brother would have gone to
England I should have been able to
avail myself of him to send to you
but he has decided to practice in
Melltown, we where all glad to hear
from you I am sorry Eliza health
is no better also of the death of her sister I remember her quite well I was
pleased to hear of all your dear Children being well and Edith such a good
girl I should like to hear from Emma
Children but I shall not write first
Since writing my last letter of Walter
broke his leg just above his ankle
he was a long time tayed up but
I am happy to say he is now quite
well and has gone to school for 2
years and is quite home for his first

Fifth letter — 18th June 1869

June 18/69

Dear Brother

Your last letter came duly to hand and I should have answered it before, but thinking Mr Hinton's brother would have gone to England I should have been able to avail myself of him to send to you, but he has disidied to practise in Melbourn. We where all glad to hear from you. I am sorry Elisa health is no better, also of the death of her sister; I remember her quite well. I was pleased to hear of all your dear children being well, and Edith such a good girl. I should like to hear from Emma children, but I shall not write first. Since writing my last letter Walter broke his leg just above the ankle. He was a long time layed up, but I am happy to say he is now quite well and has gone to school for 2 years. He is just home for his first [2] vacation. He was 14 last month.

Elizabeth has also recovered her health and is at home doing the work of the house, as I think exercise is better for her. Rosa is also quite well and send her kind love to her cousins.

William has taken a contract to supply the Angus Co/ with firewood, for the summer has been so very dry they have not been able to wash the washdirt. The rain only commenced 3 week ago, but we have all the crop in and it looks very promising. The rush that took place near us that I told you of in my last is nearly done. Where thier was a 100 men then thier is hardly one now. As soon as the winter rains sets in we shall wash our dirt up; we may get a little as the prospects where rather good. We have lost all our shares in the Star Company, as the Banks has seised it for the debt due. Thier was bad management [3] both by directors and manager. The Catherine is looking up; we have had a divident of 2% per lead[?] since I last wrote, which has made the shares a little higher in the market. We have bought 500 in the Franklin Co and I have just heard they have struck gold very heavy. I hope it is true; they are on the same line as the Angus, that company having declared 25 diffidents in 12 months. 2 years ago we where offered shares at 2/6 each, whereas at the present time they are up to 16.6 and none offering. We may have a chance yet of doing something, but in the meantime we must be thankful we do not want for the comforts of life as we have a full and plenty, although the Bank account is rather low.

vacation he was 14 last month
Elizabeth has also recovered her health
and is at home doing the work of
the house, as I think exercise is better
for her Rose is also quite well and
send her kind love to her Cousens
William has taken a Contract to supply
the Augus Co with firewood: for
the Summer has been so very dry
they have not been able to work their
work dirt the rain only commenced
3 week ago but we have all the Crops
in and it looks very promising
the rush that took place near us
that I told you of in my last
is nearly done where there was a 100
men then there is hardly one now, as
soon as the winter rains sets in we
shall wash our dirt up we may
get a little as the prospects where
rather good we have lost all our
Shares in the Star Company as the
Bankes has seesed it for the debts
due there was bad management

William earns about a pound a day with one horse and dray which is quite enough to keep us in food, for people hear is great gluttons.

[4] *Fanny and her children are well. I have not seen her; I should have gone at Chrismas to see her only for Walter accident. Your fine prince has been her again, and the whole Colony is in array agains him for applying to the English parliment for £3374.14 which he gave away in Australia, instead of which he acted with the greatest meanness. Thier was not a mine he went down but he took away all the gold he could get. I think he cleared a few thousand by the visit here, for he refused nothing; only people here was prince mad. The papers is showing him up. He is now in New Zealand.*

*My dear Brother, be sure write to me soon. The seeds came all right; they are up but I do not know if I planted to early. Rosa sends a small **parcle of gold for Edith**; she must keep it till I get a larger lot for her when you must have it made into some thing for her. They all sends thier kindest love to you and yours, and accept the same from your affectionate*

Sister Ellen Read

My good man is quite well

forth by directors and managers
the Catherine is looking up we
have had a dividend of 2½ per cent
since I last wrote which has made
the shares a little higher in the Mar
ket we have bought 500 in the
Franklin Co and I have just heard
they have struck gold very heavy
I hope it is true they ~~have~~ are
on the same line as the Augus
that Company having declared 25
dividends in 12 months 2 years
ago we were offered shares at
2/6 each whereas at the present time
~~they~~ are up to 16.6 and none offering
we may have a chance yet of do-
~~ing something but in the~~ meantime
we must be thankful we do not
want for the comforts of life as we
have a full and plenty although
the Bank account is rather low
William earns about a pound a day
with one horse and dray which is quite
enough to keep us in food for people
here is great gluttons

Notes to Fifth Letter, 18th June 1869:

At the age of forty-seven and in spite of so many pregnancies in the primitive conditions of the Bush, I suppose Ellen was now at the height of her powers. And judging from this letter they were many. She certainly seems to have 'worn the trousers': I have often wondered about the state of her marriage to a man twenty years her senior. She writes affectionately about her children and her relatives in England, but here "my good man" is referred to as an afterthought at the end of the letter. From their marriage certificate we see that he could not even sign his name, so perhaps it was inevitable that she should take the lead—even possibly feel superior.

Why ever did she marry James? To escape a lifetime of domestic service? To have the status of a married woman with her own home? Who knows? Surely had she waited she could have found someone of her own age.

It was as well that they produced most of their own food, for the speculations in various enterprises added little to their Bank account and no longer is there any suggestion of sending money home. James Read, after a very hard life, was now at sixty-nine an old man, and their eldest son William seems to have been the only bread-winner in the family.

Forty years before this, the fatherless Suter children in Portsea had to go out to work at a very early age, but delicate Elizabeth, trained as a teacher, is at home doing the housework and Walter at fourteen is still at school, and apparently boarding in Melbourne.

Ellen's brother William, now Foreman at the Standford Paper Mill, was prospering and beginning to buy property in the neighbourhood, and even lending money to other people—for interest of course. It is heart-warming to think of the paper-maker collecting seeds from his garden by the River Wey in England and sending them thousands of miles for his sister to grow in her garden in the Bush. And I wonder what happened to the 'parcel of gold'?—I have never heard the family mention it arriving in England.

Sadly Prince Alfred soon showed himself in his true colours, and has now become your "fine" Prince, understandably. What scorn there is in that word. She accuses people of being "Prince mad," but she herself was pleased to boast about being at a Reception for him to begin with, and is only being wise after the event.

Fanny and her Children are well I
have not seen her I should have gone
at Christmas to see her only for Walter
accident your fine prince has been
here again and the whole Colony is
in array against him for applying to
the English parliment for £374..14
which he gave away in frustration instead
of which he acted with the greatest mean
ness there was not a mine he went
down but he took away all the gold
he could get I think he cleared a few
thousand by the trick here for he refused
nothing only people here was never so
mad the papers is showing him up
he is now in New Zeland

My Dear Brother he sure wrote to me
soon the seeds come all right they
are up but I do not know if I planted
to early Rosa sends a small parcle
of Gold for Edith she must keep it
till I get a larger lot for her when
you must have it made into some
thing for her they all sends their
kindest love to you and yours and
accept the same from your effecnate
my good man is Sister Ellen Read
quite well

Elizabeth Read—'the flower of the flock'

Sailors Gully
January 27 / 75

My Dear Brother

You must think it
very strange that I have not
written to you before this but
I could not bring my mind
to do so trouble that I have
had since I recieved your last
letter of Eliza cliath has nearly
brougt me to death door to
commence first poor Fanny died
one year ago last June leaving
5 little children to mourn her
loss she had 4 & little girls and
she died 3 months after a birth
of a son and the 2 youngest
has died since, so the three girls
is living with their Grandmother
and is well tended to I did not
see them often for Mother in
laws in general in not very

66

Sixth letter — 27th January 1875

Sailors Gully, January 27/75
Dear Brother
You must think it very strange that I have not written to you
before this, but I could not bring my mind to do so. Trouble that I
have had since I recieved your last letter of Eliza death has nearly
brougt me to death door. To commence, first poor Fanny died one
year ago last June leaving 5 little children to mourn her loss. She
had 4 little girls and she died 3 months after a birth of a son, and the
2 youngest has died since, so the three girls is living with thier
Grandmother and is well tended to. I do not see them often for
Mother in laws in general is not very [2] amiable. But as it was, the
shock to the system brough on a severe illness, but I am thankful to
say I am much better, althoug not able to exert myself a formerly.

As for James, he has been on and of with Chronic disentry for the
last few years. We have tried all the Medical doctors avalible and
only one doctor is able to do him any good, which is a Hospital one.
We are subscribers to that institution, enables him to have advice
thier. He is now just recovering from a very bad attack, but I do not
for one moment think he can be cured as he has lived the years
allotted for man to live, as he was 74 last November.

As for business, hear it is [3] deplorable. As I now write, Bush
fires all round and water almost dried up. We have had a fearful
summer, but we must be thankful the grain was all in before the
drought set in. Thier has been a abundant harvest and food
abundant, although many a poor farmer has been burned out, and
deaths occurring with sunstrok daly.

As far as mineing is concerned, I do not like to refere to them for
they are nearly nil, but still we live in hopes of things looking better.
If it was not for Calls I could do well enough, put the Reef one in the
back ground.

unreable but as it was the shock
to the system brough on a severe
illness but I am thankful to
say I am much Better although
not able to exert myself as for
merly. as for James he has been
on and of with Chronic desentery
for the last four years we have
tried all the Medical doctors
availabe and only one doctor
is able to do him any good
which is a Hospital one we
are Subscribers to that institution
enables him to have advice
there he is now just recovering
from a very bad attact but
I do not for one moment think
he can be cured as he has lived
the years allotted for man to
live as he was 74 last November
as for business here it is

[4] *A railway of 29 miles is commencing on next Monday. The boys may get a contract on the line. I always like them to be thier own masters as they have never worke for wages, yet they are very good boys. Elizabeth is home, and tell Edith, Rose would have got her some gold but the ground is so dry; untill thier some rain she cannot find any. I have sent you my oldest son and Elizabeth likeness. When I write again you shall have Rose. I sincely trust you are all well, and write to me as soon as you can. They all join me in kindest love to the boys a Edith, from your*
    affectionate Sister

Ellen Read

deplorable as I now write Bush
fires all round and water al
most dried up we have had a
fearful Summer but we must
be thankful the grain was all
in before the drought set in
there has been a abundant
harvest and food abundant
although many a poor farmer
has been turned out, and
deaths occurring with sunstroke
daly

As far as mineing is concern
ed I do not like to refere
to them for they are nearly nil
but still we live in hopes
of things looking better if it
was not for Calls I could do
well enough but the keep me
in the back ground

Notes to Sixth Letter, 27th January 1875:

Could any two letters provide a greater contrast. In the previous one, Ellen was on top of the world—now, some five years later, she is in the depths of despair. And no wonder. To lose a child is always heart-breaking, especially so when that child leaves behind five small children of her own. When the two youngest died and the three remaining were put in the care of their paternal grandmother, Ellen's cup of bitterness over-flowed. There seems to have been little contact between the two families, for I suspect each disapproved of the marriage. From her death Certificate we learn that Fanny died of an "internal obstruction" after a very short illness.

To add to Ellen's troubles, James has developed a chronic and debilitating illness, and business is bad. Instead of their shares earning a dividend they have had to pay "calls" to help the various companies out of difficulties. She accepts her husband's illness as inevitable, since he has lived his allotted span of three score years and ten mentioned in the Bible. The weather too has conspired against them, and she herself has been ill.

Even after all these years it saddens me to think that my valiant great-great aunt had been brought so low.

In Headley, her brother William Suter's wife Eliza had died in January 1871 aged only 48. He had two teen-age sons working with him at the Mill, and his daughter Edith, at fourteen, had become his house-keeper—a responsibility she was to hold for thirty-five years— for the rest of his long life.

A railway of 29 miles is commencing on next Monday the boys may get a Contract on the line I always like them to be their own masters as they have never worked for wages yet they are very good boys Elizabeth is home and tell Edith Rose would have got her some gold but the ground is so dry untill there come rain she cannot find any I have sent you my oldest Son and Elizabeth likeness when I write again you shall have Rose I sincerely trust you are all well and write to me as soon as you can they all join me in Kindest love to the boys & Edith from your affectionate Sister
Ellen Read

Rose Read, aged about thirteen

Sailors Gully
December 27/75

My Dear Brother

I hope you have had
a Mirry Christmas and a happy
new Year, although I never saw
such plentitude in old England
as I have seen in Australia, still
what a comfort your Children
and mine has happyer days
then when we where young
of Course our Father died when
we where young which destroyed
our prospects of life, but although
so many years has elapsed I
remember as only yesterday when
Father took me and you to
Porchester Seule to see a ship that
was Burned there is not many
incidence of my Childhood but
what I remember, but your Child
dren and mine thank God has.

Seventh letter — 27th December 1875

Sailors Gully, December 27/75
My Dear Brother
I hope you have had a Merry Christmas and a happy new year, although I never seen such plentitude in old England as I have seen in Australia. Still, what a comfort your children and mine has happy days than when we where young. Of course our Father died when we where young, which destroyed our prospects of life, but although so many years has elapsed I remember as only yesterday when Father took me and you to Porchester Creek[?] to see a ship that was burned thier. Is not many incidence of my childhood but what I remember, but your children and mine thank God has [2] been spared. Our mother had a hard time to manage, but you where always a good boy to her. I may have grieved her by coming out here, but it was better than poverty. In this country one is not despised for it. I must now forget, for I am in a melancoly mood.

My son William has fenced in the ground, having a sevier winter to contend with. It has on the whole been the worse weather I have ever seen in the Colony. Even now at mid Summer we are glad of a fire and the cold is piercing. I have not sent Rose to school for the last nine months, for the unseanable weather has brough on all complaints, Measels, Scarlet fever, which Rose and Walter has not taken as yet. They now [3] are busy getting in the harvest, but rain is a great drawback. The crop on the whole looks very good, and our garden splendid. As for the gold, is only medium. If you get a little from one clame it genarly has to be payed into another in the shapes of calls, but I cannot complain; times look brisker. We have had a mery Carnibal for Chrismas. All the children was home, and Elizabeth is home for six week holidays, and this Colony is about the greates place for holidays, I think, in the world. Thier is no business done from 24 of December till the 3 of January. I shall be thankfull when it is over.

has been Spared Our Mother had
a hard time to Manage but you
where always a good boy to her
I may have grieved her by come
ing out here but it was better
than poverty, in this Country
one is not despised for it I
Must now forget for I am in
a Melancoly mood
My Son William has ferced in the
ground having a severe winter
to contend with it has on the
whole bein the worse weather I
have ever seen in the Colony
even now at mid Summer we
are glad of a fire and the cold
is piercing, I have not sent Rose
to School for the last nine Months
for the uncleanable weather has bray
on all Complaints Meusels Scarlet
fever, Which Rose and Walter has
not taken as yet they now

I have sent you Rose like- [4] ness. It is for Edith with her kindest love, but you must know she is not like her cousin, for she knows which side her bread is buttered. She does nothing in the house, not even to wash a dish or Black her Boots, and looks for a bit of gold when I commence to write. Although she has her good points, it is hard to say which is upermost. I have been ill since I wrote last, and the Old man has had another attact but is now better. The boys do not like him to do anything, but still he is plucky to the last. He thinks no one can harvest like him. He was brough up from his cradle to it, of course; he has the English stille. They all send thier kind love to you, William and Edith

from your sister

Ellen Read.

are busy getting in the harvest
but Rain is a great drawback
the Crops on the whole looks
very good, and our Garden
splendid as for the gold is
only medium if you get a
little from one claim it generaly
has to be fused into another
in the shapes of Calls but I
cannot complain times look
brisker, we have had a very
Carnival for Christmas all
the Children was home and
Elizabeth is home for six weeks
holidays and this Colony is
about the greatest place for
holidays I think in the world
there is no buisness done from
the 24 of December till the 3
of January I shall be thank
full when it is over
I have sent you Rose like

Notes to Seventh Letter, 27th December 1875:

Eleven months after the previous letter, "in a melancholy mood" after the Christmas festivities and surrounded by all the family, Ellen becomes gently nostalgic, a natural emotion at that time of year. And in other ways too, how much it echoes modern times, both in the length of the holiday and in the familiar and heartfelt cry of the harassed mother, "I shall be glad when it is all over!"

She had been four and her brother ten when their father took them to see the Man-of-War, *Diamond*, burning in Portsmouth Harbour. This was in February 1827, only two months before he died, so was probably one of their last outings together. Their mother had certainly faced a hard time after that.

"In this country one is not despised for poverty," suggests that the family back in England may have had to depend on charity, which can be a bitter and demeaning experience.

Coincidentally, it was at just this time, when the fortunes of the Suter family in Portsea were at their lowest ebb, that James Read was himself torn from his family and transported to Australia for pig stealing. But his past is never mentioned in her letters. I wonder if Ellen ever knew it?

For the first time I detect a note of pride in her husband. James had encouraged his sons to be independent and their own masters. Although living in the heart of the gold-mining area, they did not rely upon it for a living. They were self-sufficient. They held shares in several companies, but the dividends from some still had to be used to prop up others that were less successful.

There is reference once again to ill-health, but evidently Elizabeth is better, for she has been home on holiday. It seems that Ellen gets no help in the house—foolishly, perhaps to compensate for her own childhood, she has indulged Rosa to such an extent that she is a lazy and thoughtless thirteen-year-old, instead of a great help to her tired and ailing Mother.

This is the last letter we have—the last account of Ellen's life in her own words. But thanks to my friend Joyce Edwards of Canberra, and contacts that she and others have made on my behalf, I have found out more about the Read family in later years.

So, what happened next?

ness it is for Edith with her
Kindest love but you must know
she is not like her Cousin for
she knows which side her bread
is buttered she does nothing
in the house not even to wash
a dish or Black her Boots and
looks for a bit of gold when
I commence to write although she
has her good points it is hard
to say which is uppermost
I have been ill since I wrote last
and the Old man has had another
attack but is now better the
boys do not like him to
do any thing but still he is
plucky to the last he thinks
no one can harvest like him he
was brought up from his cradle
to it of Course he has the English
Still they all send their Kind
love to you William and Edith
from your sister
Ellen Read

William Suter, Ellen's brother (1817–1906)

Mrs. J. READ,
Sailors Gulley,
Bendigo
Eaglehawke Post Office
Victoria,
AUSTRALIA.

Ellen's postal address, on a slip she sent to England

Australian Postscript

Ellen Read lived for another six and a half years after writing the last letter. She died in Eaglehawk on 21st July 1882 aged 58. Her daughter Elizabeth died in the same year, aged 34.

Despite his greater age, James Read outlived his wife by five and a half years, dying on 13th February 1888 aged 87. He was survived by just three of their 14 children: William, Walter and Rose.

Rose had married Joseph Nancarrow on 13th August 1886 in Eaglehawk, and we know of at least two children being born to them: Albert Stephen (1887–1946) and Gladys May (1893–1960). Rose died in 1950. Gladys married William Bray and they had at least two children: Elsie May born 1919, and Mervyn Douglas (1920–1921).

William Read died a bachelor on 18th June 1924 aged 79. He is remembered by Hughie Harvey, an old Sailor's Gully resident, as 'a big, tall, solidly-built man, jovial and friendly, and consequently well liked'.

Walter Read is remembered by the same source as a rather taciturn man, solidly-built like his brother, a member of the Salvation Army and reputed to be an excellent draughts player. He was employed in Eaglehawk as a miner and tributed at the North Moon gold mine. (A tributor worked the ground which the company considered too dangerous to touch). He married Susan Jane Harrison, and they had six children of whom only one, Tom, survived him. Walter died on 14th May 1942 aged 84.

His son Tom, better known to all in Eaglehawk as "Tonty", was a 'good tempered, rather shambling' man who often worked at the same employment as his father, in the mines and cutting eucalyptus. He never married, and died in 1974.

William Suter, Edith's brother (1855–1904)

Full Circle

~~~
ᘐ ᘐ ᘐ
~~~

My grandfather William followed his father's trade as papermaker, living with him in the Mill House at Standford Papermill, working for the Warren family who also owned the neighbouring mill on the River Wey at Passfield.

In June 1879 he married Mary Ann Sutton, daughter of the landlord of the *Robin Hood and Little John*, one of the Standford inns. The rector, Mr WH Laverty, records in his notebook that there was 'a hitch over their marriage,' but apparently this was only because it had been planned to take place at a time which was inconvenient for him!

By the time of the 1881 census, while William senior remained in Standford with Edith as housekeeper, my grandfather and grandmother had moved to live in a third part of an old cottage in Headley High Street, which his father had bought at auction in August 1871.

And there, after a number of earlier miscarriages, my father Percy was born in July 1886. He was their only surviving child.

My grandfather continued to work in the papermills, a walk of about a mile and a half from Headley High Street, but in March 1904 he died suddenly of a heart complaint at the age of 49 years.

His father was still alive. He had moved from Standford some years previously (possibly after the Mill burned down in 1890) to live with Edith in the other end of the same cottage as his son, and outlived him by over two years, dying in December 1906 at the age of 89 years.

The Suter family was in a financial straight-jacket. My father, Percy, being 17 when his father died, was the only source of income for himself, his mother and her crippled sister Jane Sutton, and great-aunt Edith had to live on the income from William senior's property investments. When Edith finally died in 1939, she had only £30 left in her bank account.

Percy Suter (1886–1944)

My father would have liked to work with machinery, but papermaking was on the decline locally, and he ended up as a gardener. It was while gardening in Rogers' Lane (now Headley Fields) that he met my mother Nell, who was a nanny at *Lane End*. They were married at her home village of Bradwell, Buckinghamshire in October 1912, and continued to live with my widowed grandmother in Headley High Street. I was born there in June 1914.

My father died in 1944, and upon the death of my mother in 1971, the cottage in Headley High Street came into my possession, and along with it the bureau *[see photo on page 10]*—and this account of Ellen Read's life is only possible because of the discovery of her letters in it. But it had yet one more surprise to offer me.

In 1977, I decided it was time to update my insurance, and invited a valuer to assess the house contents. He reacted with amusement to the bureau. "Why do you want to keep that ugly old thing? Wouldn't the money be more useful?" He suggested I let him sell it, and suggested a reserve price of £1,000.

Of course, I readily agreed. Later that day he phoned to say that after consultation with his colleagues £3,000 seemed a more suitable amount.

An old friend and I went to Cubitt & West's Guildford Auction Rooms to find the bureau in the most prominent position and attracting much interest. It was the last item on the morning's sale:—

A WILLIAM AND MARY PERIOD FIGURED WALNUT AND FEATHER BANDED BUREAU BOOKCASE surmounted by moulded double domed cornice, the arched bevelled mirror doors enclosing two adjustable shelves and part filled interior, with candle slides below, the fall front revealing central door, pigeon holes, drawers, well, and secret drawers, the base containing concealed document slide, two short and two long drawers, 40" wide.

With open-mouthed amazement we heard the bids coming rapidly from two men just inside the door at the back of the room. They ended at £8,800 (the equivalent of about £20,000 in 2001)!

Joyce Stevens (née Suter), 1914–2007

The auctioneer's men had grinned and asked if I would like some brandy, and said they knew it would fetch a good price when the two well-known London antique dealers had appeared.

"It will soon be on its way across the Atlantic," they said.

I refused the brandy, settling instead for a quiet afternoon tea at a nearby café, and giving the waitress a tip equal to the bill. "I've just come into money," I told her.

And what a difference that windfall made to my life. For the first time, I had a nest-egg to invest—an investment which has, over the years, enabled me to remove Victorian 'improvements' from the old cottage, and restore the interior to as near its original 16th century structure as possible.

But what of the bureau? For four generations it had been in the Suter family. Where did it come from? And where is it now?

I had found several of its secret drawers and hiding places, including—after his death—one where my father had concealed a £5 note. But there were probably others.

During its time in our family it had been a very useful piece of furniture, though certainly not beautiful. I imagine it now, restored regardless of expense, its walnut and feather banding in pristine condition with the added beauty of the patina of age and installed in surroundings much more suited to its original status.

The bureau has been the beginning and the end of this story— from finding the letters which allowed me to trace the paths of the Suter family out of abject poverty, to yielding the financial support which has let me enjoy better times than most of my ancestors.

Wherever it is, in my more fanciful moments I like to think of it exerting its usual benign influence on its new owners and the people around it.

Joyce died peacefully on 12th August 2007 aged 93

The old cottage in Headley, now 'Suters'

Appendices

Appendix I—James Read

≈≈≈

Who was James Read?

Ellen Suter married James Read of Ipswich at St James Cathedral, Melbourne on 17th January 1843. He was 43 years old. But she tells us very little more about him in her letters, other than in her last where she says: *"He thinks no one can harvest like him. He was brought up from his cradle to it, of course; he has the English style."*

I have tried to find out more about him, and discovered that a James Read of the right age was sentenced in Suffolk to transportation for 7 years for 'grand larceny—stealing a pig.

He arrived in Australia on the ship *Phoenix* on 14th July 1828 which had sailed from Spithead. His convict record reads as follows:

James Read. Tried: Bury, 18th October 1826. Offence: Pig stealing. Previous Convictions: None. Sentence: 7 years. Age & Condition: 27 years; married with 2 children. Education: Read & write. Religion: Protestant. Native Place: Suffolk. Trade or Calling: Ploughman. Description: 5'–5¼"; ruddy florid complexion; brown hair; hazel eyes; small mark of cut on right side of upper lip. How disposed of: Wm Balcombe Esq., Sydney. *(Ref: Archives Office of NSW).*

Although this record says he could read and write, he still only 'made his mark' on his marriage certificate in 1843.

He doesn't appear in the 1837 Muster for NSW, but by this time he should have finished his sentence.

Appendix II—Ellen's children

ⁿⓞⓛ ⓞⓛ ⓞⓛ

How many children did Ellen & James Read have, and when?

When Ellen died, there were fourteen children listed on her death certificate—but their details do not tally entirely with other sources. She wrote in 1867: *"Only five out of 14 alive ... I had twins three times running, all have died but [Rose]."*
As far as I can ascertain, her children in sequence of birth were:—

- **William James**, born 1845 at Ovens River, NSW; registered at St James, Melbourne; died 1924 aged 79 (unmarried)

- Two stillbirths (unnamed)

- **Frances Emma (Fanny)**, born 1847 at Goulburn River, NSW; registered at St James, Melbourne; married Charles Cook 1866; died 1873 at Eaglehawk aged 27, leaving 5 children

- **Elizabeth Susan**, born 1848; died 1882 aged 34 (unmarried)

- **John Suter**, born 1850; died between 1853 & 1867 (ie. the dates of the first two letters), and probably before Walter was born in 1857, since he also was given the names John Suter

- **George Edwin**, died before 1853

- **Walter John Suter**, born 1855 (though Ellen's death certificate lists him as the twin of Ada Louise—he was also said to be aged 14 in Ellen's letter of May 1867); married; died 1942 aged 87 leaving one son

- **Ada Louise** (twin), born Oct 1857; died at Skinflint Gully Apr 1863 aged 5½ (on death certificate)

- **Arthur Benjamin**, assumed to be the twin born with Ada Louise in 1857, died

- **James** (twin), born Nov 1860, died at Benella aged 4 months

- **Alice Ellen** (twin), born Nov 1860, died at Benella, 3 weeks

- **Rosetta (Rosa, Rose)** (twin) born 1862; married 1886 to James Nancarrow and had children

- **Lilian**, assumed to be the twin born with Rose in 1862, died soon after.

Appendix III — Calendar of Events

⟳⟳⟳

1800   Nov: James READ born (in Ipswich)

1815   May 18: William SUTER marries Frances CHIVERTON at
       St Mary, Portsea

1816   Jan 28: Amelia SUTER (Ellen's sister) baptised (St John,
       Portsea) living at Marlborough Row
       Oct 28: Mahala (Amelia?) SUTER buried age 9 months,
       living at Unicorn Street

1817   Feb 25: William SUTER (Ellen's brother) born in Portsea
       (bapt St Mary 16 Mar 1817) living at Britain Street

1819   Mar 4: Emma SUTER (Ellen's sister) baptised (St John,
       Portsea) living at Pollard Court

1822   Feb 23: Helen (Ellen) SUTER born in Portsea (bapt St Mary
       17 Aug 1823) living at Gloucester Street

1826   Oct 18: James READ, age 27, of Letheringham, Suffolk
       convicted of pig-stealing at Bury St. Edmunds—sentence
       seven years transportation—he is married with 2 children

1827   Feb 18: HMS *Diamond* catches fire at night moored in
       Portsmouth Harbour
       May: William SUTER (Ellen's father) dies age 43
       Jun 28: Twins Edwin & Emma Ann SUTER baptised (St
       John, Portsea) living at Gloucester Street

1828   Jul 14: James READ arrives in NSW as a convict on the
       Phoenix
       Oct 29: Edwin SUTER buried age 16 months (St Mary,
       Portsea)

1841   Apr 4: *Westminster* leaves Gravesend
       Apr 17: *Westminster* leaves Plymouth for Australia – Ellen
       SUTER on board
       June 16: UK Census: William SUTER (25) papermaker in
       Standford, Headley, near to Joseph HOWARD (75)
       papermaker and his wife Sarah HOWARD (65)—'Fanny'
       SUTER (46) nurse in the household of William Chiverton of
       Carisbrooke, Isle of Wight
       July 29: Ellen SUTER aged 19 years arrives in Australia
       (Port Phillip) after 104 days on *Westminster*

1842   Jun 2: Sarah HOWARD dies in Standford

1843   Jan 17: Ellen SUTER marries James READ at St James Cathedral, Melbourne—he a bachelor of Ovens River, she 'of this parish'
Feb 2: Ellen's mother Frances SUTER re-marries, to Joseph HOWARD of Standford
Aug 21: Joseph HOWARD dies

1845   William James READ born to Ellen at Ovens River, NSW

1846   Jul 27: Emma SUTER of King St, Southsea marries Charles Rishman BAKER

1847   Frances Emma [Fanny] READ born to Ellen at Ovens River, NSW (baptised 1857)
Jul 15: William SUTER (Ellen's brother) marries Eliza CHIVERTON in Carisbrooke, Isle of Wight

1848   Mar 21: Frances HOWARD (née SUTER) re-marries again (to William BARNETT, at Ebenezer Baptist Chapel, Portsea)
Elizabeth Susan READ born to Ellen (at Ovens River?)

1849   Ellen sends a £40 Bill of Exchange to her mother—receives no reply

1850   John Suter READ born to Ellen

1851   Mar 30 Headley census: William SUTER (34, paper finisher journeyman) and Eliza SUTER (30, paper sorter) in Standford; William BARNETT (57, Ag Lab) & Frances BARNETT (58) in Arford
Victoria splits from New South Wales

1852   Jan: Ellen sends another £40 Bill of Exchange to her mother—again receives no reply
April: First nugget found at Eaglehawk – within 3 years the population rises to 20,000
Apr 19: George SUTER born to William & Eliza in Headley
George Edwin READ born to Ellen (died prior to July 1853)
First voyage of SS 'Great Britain' to Australia – reduced travel time significantly

1853   July 20: [See first letter] Ellen (age 31) writes fifteenth letter to her family in 12 months – all previously unanswered. Only one letter received in 12 years. *"William my eldest boy is just eight year old and is getting on very fast; Fanny is seven years old, a curly head fat girl very strong but bids fare to be very promising; Elizabeth is five years next month, a little tiny thing but a general favourite and pronounced to be the flower of the flock; John Suter is three years my youngest alive"*

1855	Mar 29: William SUTER born to William & Eliza in Headley
	May: Walter John Suter READ born to Ellen
1856	*Wooden classroom built in Eaglehawk*
1857	*Aug 1: Eaglehawk Post Office opens*
	Oct?: Ada Louise [and Arthur Benjamin?] READ born to Ellen in Skinflint Gully
1858	Apr 13: Edith SUTER born to William & Eliza in Headley (baptised 1874)
1860	*April 1: Presbyterian Church opens in Eaglehawk*
	Nov: Alice Ellen & James READ (twins) born to Ellen (at Skinflint Gully?)
	Dec 28: Alice Ellen READ buried at Benella, Broken River aged 5 weeks
1861	Apr 2: James READ buried at Benella aged 4 months
	Apr 7: Headley census: William (44, paper maker foreman), Eliza (39, paper bag maker), George (8), William (5) and Edith (2) SUTER, all in Standford
1862	Oct 9: Rosetta [Rose] & Lilian READ (twins) born to Ellen (at Skinflint Gully?) – Lilian dies
	Eaglehawk declared a municipality
1863	Apr 11: Frances BARNETT (Ellen's mother) buried in Headley, age 67
	April 23: Ada Louise READ dies, age 5½
	May 26: St Peter's Anglican Church opens at Eaglehawk
186?	Emma BAKER (née SUTER) dies in England
1866	Jun 4: Fanny READ marries Charles COOK of Tocumwal at St Peter's Eaglehawk
1867	Jan 26: [See second letter] Ellen (age 44) writes to her brother – sad to hear of the death of her Mother and of Emma – *"sorry to hear Eliza is not in good health" – "on the 23 of next month I shall be 45 years old" – "my good man was sixty six last November and strong and hale" – "Elizabeth sends her kind love to all her Cousins. She is 18 years old and does all my housework" – "Our pet Rosa says she wants to see her cousin Edith; she is four years old and the last of six. I had twins 3 times running, all have died but her" – "I have had my trouble losing so many children; only five out of 14 alive"*
	May 19: Emma Ada born to Fanny COOK (née READ) in Eaglehawk (came down from the Murray to be confined)

Sept 26: [See third letter] Ellen writes long letter to her brother – *"Elizabeth went to Melbourne in January last to pass an examination as a Teacher for the National School Eaglehawk she was down three months and obtained a second class Certificate"* – *"I sent you a paper in May last announcing the birth of Fanny baby which was born at Eaglehawk on the 19th May"* – *"Rose is so pleased with Edith for sending the picture"* – *"Walter wishes he could be in England only to see snow"* – *"My boys are quite well and still going on with their contract which is nearly done. The Catherine Reef is doing very well but no yet declared a dividend."* – *"You may depend the Colony is quite mad respecting the arrival of Prince Alfred"*

Dec 18: Prince Alfred, Duke of Edinburgh, visits Bendigo

1868   *Mar 12: Henry James O'Farrell shot at Prince Alfred in Sydney—hanged Apr 21*

Aug: Frances Sarah born to Fanny COOK (née READ)

Sep 10: [See fourth letter] Ellen writes to her brother – *"I did not receive your letter of February until July do not send any more letters by the Panama route"* – *"we have received your Prince and sent him home shot"* – *"Things begin to look a little brighter, the Catherine is looking up, the Crushing last fortnight was 300 ounces, the whole of the debt at the bank is payed off, the shares is rising in the market, if they go on this way we shall soon have a return"*

1869   Martha born to Fanny COOK (née READ)

June 18: [See fifth letter] Ellen writes to her brother – *"Walter broke his leg just above the ankle he was a long time layed up but I am happy to say he is now quite well and has gone to school for two years he is just home for his first vacation he was 14 last month"* – *"Elizabeth has also recovered her health and is at home doing the work of the house"* – *"William has taken a contract to supply the Angus Co/ with Firewood for the summer"* – *"Fanny and her children are well"* – *"your fine prince has been her again and the whole Colony is in array against him – their was not a mine he went down but he took away all the gold he could get"*

Nov 18: Suez Canal opens, speeding steam travel between Britain and Australia

1870   Susan born to Fanny COOK (née READ) at Albury, NSW

1871   Jan 20: Eliza SUTER of Standford, wife of William, buried at Headley age 48

Jan 21: William BARNETT, 3rd husband of Frances SUTER, buried at Headley age 84

Apr 2: Headley census: William (paper maker foreman, 53, wid), George (paper maker finisher, 18), William (paper finisher, 16), Edith (scholar, 12) SUTER, all in Standford

Aug 9: William SUTER buys '3 tenements' in Headley—the old cottage in the High Street later to become *Suters*

1873   Apr: Charles James born to Fanny COOK (née READ)

Jun 17: Fanny COOK (née READ) dies of intestinal obstruction, age 27, leaving 5 children (buried Eaglehawk)

Dec 21: Susan COOK dies age 3

1874   Jan 14: Charles James COOK dies age 9 months

1875   Jan 27: [See sixth letter] Ellen writes to her brother – *"You must think it very strange that I have not written to you before this but I could not bring my mind to do so trouble that I have had"* – *"poor Fanny died one year ago last June having 5 little children to mourn her loss"* – *"Bush fires all round and water almost dried up we have had a fearful summer"* – *"A railway of 29 miles is coming in next Monday"*

Dec 27: [See seventh letter] Ellen (age 53) writes to her brother – *"My son William has fenced in the ground having a severe winter to contend with; it has on the whole been the worst weather I have ever seen in the Colony, even now at mid Summer we are glad of a fire and the cold is piercing, I have not sent Rose to school for the last nine months"* – *"Rose and Walter are now getting in the harvest but rain is a great drawback"* – *"Elizabeth is home for six week holidays"*

1879   Jun 25: William SUTER marries Mary Ann SUTTON in Headley

1881   Apr: Headley census: William (papermaker, 63), Edith (dau, housekeeper, 22) SUTER in Standford; William (papermaker, 26) & Mary Ann (wife, 25) SUTER in Headley High Street

1882   July 21: Ellen READ (née SUTER) dies in Eaglehawk of a stroke, age 58

Elizabeth READ dies

1883   Apr 10: Stillbirth to William & Mary SUTER in Headley

1885   Jul 7: Another stillbirth to William & Mary SUTER in Headley

1886   Jul 3: Percy born to William & Mary SUTER in Headley

	Aug 23: Rose READ (22) marries Joseph NANCARROW, miner, at Eaglehawk
1887	Albert Stephen NANCARROW born
	Nov 14: Charles COOK dies
1888	Feb 13: James READ dies age 87 (William, Walter & Rose survive him)
1890	Martha COOK dies age 21
1891	Apr 5: Headley census: William (retd papermaker, 74), Edith (dau, housekeeper, 34) SUTER; William (papermaker, 36), Mary Ann (wife, 35), Percy (son, 4) SUTER, all in Headley High Street
	Name of Sandhurst, Victoria, changed by poll to Bendigo
1893	May 1: Gladys May NANCARROW born
1895	Thomas Edgar READ born to Walter and Susan
1896	William SUTER (elder) has two cottages built in Headley Fields for £320
1904	Mar 29: Younger William SUTER dies in Headley of 'heart & dropsy' age 49
1906	Dec 11: Elder William SUTER dies in Headley age 89
1912	Oct 26: Percy SUTER marries Nellie Mary SEAR at Bradwell, Bucks
1914	Jun 22: Joyce Mary Eileen born to Percy & Nellie SUTER in Headley
1924	June 18: William James READ dies in Eaglehawk age 79, unmarried
1939	Jan 8: Edith SUTER dies in Headley age 81, unmarried
1942	Feb 4: Mary Ann SUTER dies in Headley age 86
	May 14: Walter John Suter READ dies in Bendigo age 87 (widower of Susan Jane HARRISON — 4 children, one surviving: Thomas Edgar READ, then aged 47)
1944	Dec 8: Percy SUTER dies, age 58
2007	Aug 12: Joyce STEVENS (née SUTER) dies age 93

ⱳⱳⱳ

Acknowledgements

My thanks to the following individuals who have been kind enough to help me in my search for information, over a considerable number of years in some cases.

Jill Chambers, Gaye Dwyer, Joyce Edwards, Anna Ide,
Betty Jackman, Dot Skewes, Doreen Smith,
John Owen Smith, Ray Wallace.

I also consulted the following general texts:—

The Somerset Years by Florence Chuk;
The Long Farewell by Don Charlwood.

Other books relating to the history of Headley

❧ ❧ ❧

One Monday in November...and Beyond
—*the story of the Selborne and Headley Workhouse Riots of 1830*
During the 'Swing' riots of 1830, according to the famed historians
J.L. and Barbara Hammond, "the most interesting event in the
Hampshire rising was the destruction of the workhouses at Selborne
and Headley." If these riots had succeeded, "the day when the
Headley workhouse was thrown down would be remembered ... as
the day of the taking of the Bastille." Here a local historian traces the
dramatic events of two days of rioting and its aftermath in the villages
and beyond. *ISBN 978-1-873855-33-1 August 2002, paperback,
130pp, illustrations plus maps.*

All Tanked Up—*the Canadians in Headley during World War II*
A story of the benign 'invasion' of Headley by Canadian tank
regiments over a period of four years, told from the point of view of
both Villagers and Canadians. Includes many personal reminiscences
and illustrations. *ISBN 978-1-873855-00-3 May 1994, paperback,
48pp, illustrations plus maps.*

To the Ar and Back—*an historical stroll around Headley and Arford*
Joyce Stevens tells us the history of forty-seven locations within a
mile of the centre of Headley. Illustrated with line drawings by Mick
Borra. *The Headley Society, updated 2006, paperback, 26pp,
illustrations plus map.*

Headley's Past in Pictures — *a tour of the parish in old photographs*
Headley as it was in the first half of the 20th century. In this book
you are taken on an illustrated tour of the parish by means of three
journeys – the first around the centre of Headley and Arford, the
second to Headley Down and beyond, and the third along the River
Wey and its tributaries. In doing so, we venture occasionally outside
today's civil parish boundaries – but that too is all part of the history
of Headley. *ISBN 978-1-873855-27-0 December 1999, updated
2003, over 100 photographs, plus historical notes and maps of area.*

/contd ...

On the Trail of Flora Thompson—*beyond Candleford Green*
The author of *Lark Rise to Candleford* worked in Grayshott post
office from 1898–1901, while it was still in the parish of Headley.
A local historian investigates the people and places she would have
seen here at that time. *ISBN 978-1-873855-24-9 First published May
1997, updated 2005, paperback, 144pp, illustrations plus maps.*

Heatherley—*by Flora Thompson*—*her sequel to the 'Lark Rise'
trilogy.* This is the book which Flora Thompson wrote about her time
in Grayshott. It is the 'missing' fourth part to her *Lark Rise to
Candleford* in which 'Laura Goes Further.' Full of interest to those
who know this area. Illustrated with chapter-heading line drawings
by Hester Whittle. Introduction by Ann Mallinson.
*ISBN 978-1-873855-29-4 Sept 1998, paperback, 178pp, illustrations
plus maps.*

Grayshott—*the story of a Hampshire village*—*J.H. (Jack) Smith*
The history of Grayshott from its earliest beginnings as a minor
hamlet of Headley to its status as a fully independent parish
flourishing on (and across) the borders of Hampshire and Surrey.
*ISBN 978-1-873855-38-6 First published 1976, republished 2002,
illustrated*

Churt: a Medieval Landscape—*by Philip Brooks*—A remarkable
insight into the world of ox plough teams, hand-sown crops and a
community whose very survival was dependent on the produce of the
land. *ISBN 978-1-873855-52-2 First published 2000, republished
2006, illustrated.*

I'Anson's Chalet on Headley Hill—*a hidden house, a hidden
history*—Hidden among the pine trees on Headley Hill there is a
Swiss-style chalet. Who built it and why? Judith Kinghorn
investigates the history of her house, now called *Windridge*, and
discovers a fascinating cast of characters.
ISBN 978-1-873855-48-5 October 2004, illustrated.

John Owen Smith, publisher:—
Tel/Fax: (01428) 712892
E-mail: wordsmith@headley-village.com
Web Site: www.headley-village.com/wordsmith